Grosset & Dunlap

Library of Congress Cataloging-in-Publication Data

Penner, Lucille Recht.
Cowboys / by Lucille Recht penner; illustrated by Ben Carter.
p. cm. —
1. Cowboys—West (U.S.)—Juvenile literature. 2. West (U.S.)—Social life and customs—Juvenile literature.
3. Frontier and pioneer life—West (U.S.)—Juvenile literature. [1. Cowboys. 2. West (U.S.)—Social life and customs.] I. Carter, Ben, ill. II. Title. III. Series.
F596.P455 1995
978—dc20 94-35463
CIP
AC

ISBN 0-448-40947-X F G H I J

COWBOYS

By Lucille Recht Penner
Illustrated by Ben Carter

Grosset & Dunlap, Publishers

If you were out west about a hundred years ago, you might have heard a cowboy yelling—ti yi yippy yay!—as he rode across the plains.

What was it like to be a cowboy way back then?

Cowboys lived on cattle ranches. A ranch had a house for the rancher and his family, barns for animals, and a bunkhouse where the cowboys slept. The rancher owned thousands of cattle. They wandered for miles looking for grass and water.

Twice a year, the cowboys drove all the cattle together. This was called a roundup. The cowboys counted the baby calves that had been born since the last roundup. The biggest cattle were chosen to sell at market.

A roundup was hard work. The cattle were wild and fast. They had long, sharp, dangerous horns. Cowboys called them Longhorns. If you made a Longhorn mad, it would charge at you. A cowboy didn't want to get close to an angry Longhorn.

So he made a loop in the end of his rope. Then he twirled it over his head and let it fly. When he caught the Longhorn, he could tell that it belonged to his ranch.

How could he tell? It was easy. Each rancher put a special mark called a brand on his cows. Baby calves didn't have brands, yet. They didn't need them. A baby calf always followed its mother.

Every ranch had its own name and its own brand. The Rocking Chair Ranch brand looked like a rocking chair. The Flying V Ranch brand looked like this:

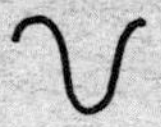

After the roundup was over, it was time to sell the Longhorns. That meant taking them to big market towns. Back then, there were no roads across the wide plains—only dusty trails that cattle had made with their hooves as they tramped along. Some trails were a thousand miles long! Since cattle could walk only fifteen miles a day, the long, hard trip often lasted months. It was called a trail drive. There was a lot to do to get ready.

At the beginning of a trail drive, one cowboy rode out in front of the herd. "Come on, boys," he called to the cattle. A few big Longhorns started after him. They bellowed and swung their heads from side to side. Other cattle followed, and soon they were all on their way.

Cattle didn't like so much walking. After a while, they wanted to turn around and go home. Cowboys rode up and down the sides of the herd to keep them in line. A few cowboys rode at the end of the herd to make sure no cattle were left behind.

It was hot on the trail. Cowboys wore hats with wide brims to keep the sun out of their eyes. When it rained, the brims made good umbrellas. Around their necks, cowboys wore red bandannas. When it got dusty, they pulled the bandannas over their noses. Leather leggings—called chaps—were tied over their pants to keep out thorns and cactus spines.

High leather boots kept out dirt and pebbles. Cowboy boots had handles called "mule ears." The cowboy grabbed the mule ears to pull his boots off and on.

What else did a cowboy need on the trail? A good horse. Cowboys spent the whole day on horseback. They rode little horses called cow ponies. A good cow pony was fearless. It could cross rough ground in the blackest night. It could swim a deep, wide river.

It could crash right through the bushes after a runaway cow. The cowboy had to hold on tight!

Every day the herd tramped the hot, dry plains. Two or three big steers were the leaders. They always walked in front. The cowboys got to know them well. They gave them pet names, like "Old Grumpy" and "Starface."

Cows could get in trouble. Sometimes one got stuck in the mud. The cowboy roped it and pulled it out. A cow might get hurt on the trail. A cowboy took care of that, too.

At night the cowboys stopped to let the cattle eat, drink, and sleep. It was time for the cowboys to eat, too. "Cookie" had a hot meal ready for them. That's what cowboys called the cook.

Cookie drove a special wagon called the chuckwagon. It had drawers for flour, salt, beans, and pots and pans. A water barrel was tied underneath.

Cookie gave every cowboy a big helping of biscuits, steak, gravy, and beans. He cooked the same meal almost every night, but the cowboys didn't mind. It tasted good!

There were no tables or chairs, so the cowboys sat right on the ground. After dinner they played cards or read by the flickering light of the campfire. The nights were chilly and bright with stars.

But the cowboys didn't stay up late. They were tired. At bedtime, they just pulled off their boots and crawled into their bedrolls. A cowboy never wore pajamas. What about a pillow? He used his saddle.

Trail drives were dangerous. Many things could go wrong.

The herd might stampede if there was a loud noise—like a sudden crash of thunder. A stampede was scary. Cattle ran wildly in all directions, rolling their eyes and bellowing with fear. The ground shook under them. The bravest cowboys galloped to the front of the herd. They had to make the leaders turn. They shouted at them and fired their six-shooters in the air. They tried to make the cattle run in a circle until they calmed down.

Sometimes they'd run into rustlers. A rustler was a cow thief. Rustlers hid behind rocks and jumped out at the cattle to make them stampede. While the cowboys were trying to catch the terrified cattle and calm them down, the rustlers drove off as many as they could.

When the herd came to a big river, the cowboys in front galloped right into the water. The cattle plunged in after them. The cattle swam mostly under water. Sometimes the cowboys could see only the tips of their black noses and their long white horns.

Most cowboys didn't know how to swim. If a cowboy fell into the water, he grabbed his horse's tail and held on tight until they reached shore.

Trail drives often went through Indian Territory. The Indians charged ten cents a head to let the cattle cross their land. If the cowboys didn't pay, there might be a fight. But usually the money was handed over and the herd plodded on.

At last, the noisy, dusty cattle stamped into a market town. The cowboys drove them into pens near the railroad tracks. Then they got their pay. It was time for fun!

What do you think most cowboys wanted first? A bath! The barber had a big tub in the back of the shop. For a dollar, you could soak and soak. A boy kept throwing in pails of hot water. Ahh-h-h! Next it was time for a shave, a haircut, and some new clothes.

Tonight, the cowboys would sleep in real beds and eat dinner at a real table. They would sing, dance, and have fun with their friends.

But soon they would be heading back to Longhorn country. There would be many more hot days in the saddle. There would be many more cold nights under the stars.